"The St. Louis Blues"
and Other Song Hits of 1914

Edited by
SANDY MARRONE

DOVER PUBLICATIONS, INC., NEW YORK

ACKNOWLEDGMENTS

The publisher is grateful to David A. Jasen for lending the original sheet music of "Goodbye, Girls, I'm Through," "He's a Rag Picker," "The St. Louis Blues" and "They Didn't Believe Me." "Wien, du Stadt meiner Träume" was kindly loaned by the Sibley Music Library of the Eastman School of Music, Rochester, N.Y.

All other songs were provided by Sandy Marrone.

Copyright © 1990 by Dover Publications, Inc.
All rights reserved under Pan American and
International Copyright Conventions.

Published in Canada by General Publishing Company, Ltd.,
30 Lesmill Road, Don Mills, Toronto, Ontario.
Published in the United Kingdom by Constable and Company, Ltd.,
10 Orange Street, London WC2H 7EG.

"The St. Louis Blues" and Other Song Hits of 1914 is a new work, first published by Dover Publications, Inc., in 1990. It consists of unabridged, unaltered republications of the sheet music of 21 popular songs (original publishers and dates of publication are indicated in the Contents), as well as a new Publisher's Note, Notes on the Song Texts and Alphabetical List of Songwriters and Lyricists.

Manufactured in the United States of America
Dover Publications, Inc.
31 East 2nd Street
Mineola, N.Y 11501

Library of Congress Cataloging-in-Publication Data

The St. Louis blues and other song hits of 1914.

For voice and piano.
Reproduced from the original sheet music eds.
1. Popular music—1911–1920.   I. Marrone, Sandy.
II. Title.   III. Title: St. Louis blues.
M1630.18.S782   1990   89-755377
ISBN 0-486-26383-5

Publisher's Note

THE 21 SONGS in the present album, all remembered and frequently performed today, were products of a single rich year, 1914. The volume is named for the outstanding song of the year, which quickly became a worldwide favorite. Arranged and adapted so very often, "The St. Louis Blues" may not be known to its many admirers in its absolutely original published form, as presented here. W. C. Handy's classic, which followed closely upon his epoch-making "The Memphis Blues" (piano version, 1912; song version, 1913), is a fascinating amalgam of different verbal and musical patterns from Southern oral tradition. Its first section begins in a frequently occurring blues form (12-bar theme, the text of the 12 bars being a couplet with its first line repeated), then (at the words "St. Louis 'oman") moves into a more pop-style 16-bar passage with a tango-like accompaniment. The final section (at the words "Got de St. Louis Blues") returns to the 12-bar pattern in the music, but the text consists of three different lines, all rhyming. As stated in the published piece, the strain of the last section had been used earlier in Handy's "The Jogo Blues," an instrumental piece published in 1913.

Another star composer of 1914, represented here by five great numbers, was Irving Berlin, who had begun his career auspiciously in 1907 and was never to look back. His 1914 ragtime songs frequently show him breaking new ground compositionally, loosening rigid Tin Pan Alley frameworks with many kinds of inventive variations, large and small. A couple of examples will suffice. The vigorously syncopated "This Is the Life" has an almost completely free structure. In "He's a Rag Picker" there is no formal "release" section, and when the main theme returns (at the words "makes an ordinary ditty"), it is broken into shorter notes and occurs in the middle of a sentence. But the foremost Berlin experiment of the year—and a completely successful one—is "Play a Simple Melody," the first of several hits by this composer in which there are two independent melodies that can be sung together. The introduction ("verse") to this song is written in a sophisticated style redolent of the influential British musicals of the period (recitative-like music with elevated vocabulary). Since the song was composed for a Broadway show—the first ever with a full Berlin score—this sophistication exemplifies its author's constant adaptability to new situations and demands, an aspect of his talent that was to flower more and more in the next years. Incidentally, the commercial shrewdness of appealing to two audiences (lovers of either old-fashioned tunes or rag) inherent in "Play a Simple Melody" is also evident in the fact that Berlin could simultaneously turn out with equal ease a celebration for city dwellers of life back on the farm ("I Want to Go Back to Michigan") and a paean to city life for farmers ("This Is the Life").

Jerome Kern is triumphantly represented here by two songs written to be interpolated into other composers' shows, especially British imports that seemed to need a Yankee shot in the arm. (This extremely frequent practice of the time foreshadowed the later Hollywood syndrome of buying a Broadway show and then junking all or most of the original score.) Up to 1914, the year of this anthology, Kern wrote interpolations almost exclusively; this situation was to change drastically and permanently in 1915, when he launched his famous series of Princess Theatre shows. Both "You're Here and I'm Here" and "They Didn't Believe Me" are fresh-sounding and elegantly constructed numbers. In the former song, the second entry of the main theme, after the middle section, suggests a modulation to a new key; and the tiny filler (at the words "It would be heaven"), introduced seemingly gratuitously just before that second entry, later provides the closing formula of the song (at the words "a little cosy corner"). It is amusing to note that, in view of the continuing dance craze of that era (notice the big play given to the Castles), the publisher included a second set of words that mentions, or puns upon, such popular dances as tangos, glides and hesitation waltzes. "They Didn't Believe Me" contains a passage, unusual at the time and criticized by some for banality, that is customarily sung nowadays as "And I'm certainly going to tell them." The awkward original wording, as reproduced here, may come as a surprise to many: "And I certn'ly am goin' to tell them."

Other 1914 entries can be discussed more briefly. Victor Herbert contributed a magnificent waltz that year, "When You're Away." Percy Wenrich, continuing to uphold old-time, homey values in a raggedy age, gave us "When You Wore a Tulip." Ernest Ball provided another Irish-American classic in "A Little Bit of Heaven." "The Missouri Waltz" became a favorite of President Truman and the state song of Missouri. Note that the lyricist is also the writer of "Too-Ra-Loo-Ra-Loo-Ral," yet another Irish-American number in this volume. The First World War began to impinge slightly on U.S. consciousness with a novelty tongue twister popularized here by Al Jolson, "Sister Susie's Sewing Shirts for Soldiers." Just the first three notes of the refrain of "By the Beautiful Sea," whenever they appear in a background score, evoke seaside resorts and pleasures for the American public. This emblematic status is surely what the writers (and energetic pluggers) intended to achieve from the outset, since the number was clearly inspired by an earlier British counterpart that does just the same for Britishers, "I Do Like to Be Beside the Seaside" (1909). The lyrics of the last few bars of the two songs are particularly close. The other American songs in the volume are self-explanatory.

Probably the most unusual item in this book is a Viennese waltz song, "Wien, du Stadt meiner Träume," in its original German-language version (1914). American versions were not written until years later ("Someone Will Make You Smile," 1923; "Vienna Dreams," 1937), but the piece is so fine (and so famous now) that its inclusion here, even in German, seemed warranted and desirable. A literal translation of the full German text will be found, along with other material, in the section "Notes on the Song Texts" on page ix. The "Alphabetical List of Songwriters and Lyricists" on page vii includes brief biographical data.

Contents

The songs are arranged in alphabetical order, using their titles as printed either on the first page of music of the original sheets or else on the cover [exception: "Play a Simple Melody," alphabetized under P through the force of tradition], and not counting "A" or "The" at the beginning of the title. The publishers given here (abbreviated "Pub.") are those indicated on the covers of the specific first or early editions being reprinted. The years given are those of copyright.

The Aba Daba Honeymoon   1
  Words & music: Arthur Fields & Walter Donovan. Pub.: Leo. Feist, Inc., N.Y, 1914.

By the Beautiful Sea   6
  Words: Harold R. Atteridge. Music: Harry Carroll. Pub.: Shapiro, Bernstein & Co., Inc., N.Y, 1914.

By the Waters of Minnetonka (Moon Dear)   11
  Words: J. M. Cavanass. Music: Thurlow Lieurance. Pub.: Theodore Presser Co., Philadelphia, 1914. (Originally published in the album *Indian Songs*; the cover reproduced here is from a later separate printing.)

Can't Yo' Heah Me Callin' (Caroline)   17
  Words: William H. Gardner. Music: Caro Roma. Pub.: M. Witmark & Sons, N.Y, 1914.

Down on the Farm: *see* I Want to Go Back to Michigan

Goodbye, Girls, I'm Through   22
  From the musical *Chin-Chin*. Words: John Golden. Music: Ivan Caryll. Pub.: Chappell & Co. Ltd., N.Y, 1914.

He's a Devil in His Own Home Town   28
  Words: Grant Clarke & Irving Berlin. Music: Irving Berlin. Pub.: Waterson, Berlin & Snyder Co., N.Y, 1914.

He's a Rag Picker   32
  Words & music: Irving Berlin. Pub.: Waterson, Berlin & Snyder Co., N.Y, 1914.

Hush-a-bye, Ma Baby: *see* (The) Missouri Waltz

I Want to Go Back to Michigan (Down on the Farm)   37
  Words & music: Irving Berlin. Pub.: Waterson, Berlin & Snyder Co., N.Y, 1914.

A Little Bit of Heaven (Shure They Call It Ireland)   42
  From the play with songs *The Heart of Paddy Whack*. Words: J. Keirn Brennan. Music: Ernest R. Ball. Pub.: M. Witmark & Sons, N.Y, 1914.

The Missouri Waltz (Hush-a-bye, Ma Baby)   47
  Words: J. R. Shannon. Music: "from an Original Melody procured by John Valentine Eppel, Arr[anged] for piano by Frederic Knight Logan." Pub.: F. J. A. Forster, Chicago, 1914.

Moon Dear: *see* By the Waters of Minnetonka

Play a Simple Melody (Simple Melody; Won't You Play a Simple Melody)   53
  From the musical *Watch Your Step*. Words & music: Irving Berlin. Pub.: Irving Berlin Inc., N.Y, 1914.

The St. Louis Blues   57
    Words & music: W. C. Handy. Pub.: The Pace & Handy Music Co., Memphis, 1914.

Simple Melody: *see* Play a Simple Melody

Sister Susie's Sewing Shirts for Soldiers   62
    Words: R. P. Weston. Music: Hermann E. Darewski. Pub.: T. B. Harms and Francis, Day & Hunter, N.Y, 1914.

Sylvia   67
    Words: Clinton Scollard. Music: Oley Speaks. Pub.: G. Schirmer, N.Y, 1914.

That's an Irish Lullaby: *see* Too-Ra-Loo-Ra-Loo-Ral

They Didn't Believe Me   71
    Interpolated in the New York production of the 1913 British musical *The Girl from Utah*. Words: Herbert Reynolds. Music: Jerome (D.) Kern. Pub.: T. B. Harms and Francis, Day & Hunter, N.Y, 1914.

This Is the Life   76
    Words & music: Irving Berlin. Pub.: Waterson, Berlin & Snyder Co., N.Y, 1914.

Too-Ra-Loo-Ra-Loo-Ral (That's an Irish Lullaby)   81
    From the play with songs *Shameen Dhu*. Words & music: J. R. Shannon. Pub.: M. Witmark & Sons. The 1913 copyright was apparently for a professional edition only, the first regular edition being 1914, when the play opened.

When You're Away   85
    From the musical *The Only Girl*. Words: Henry Blossom. Music: Victor Herbert. Pub.: M. Witmark & Sons, N.Y, 1914.

When You Wore a Tulip (and I Wore a Big Red Rose)   90
    Words: Jack Mahoney. Music: Percy Wenrich. Pub.: Leo. Feist, Inc., N.Y, 1914.

Wien, du Stadt meiner Träume   94
    Words & music: Rudolf Sieczyński. Pub.: Adolf Robitschek, Vienna, 1914.

Won't You Play a Simple Melody: *see* Play a Simple Melody

You're Here and I'm Here   99
    Interpolated in the New York production of *The Marriage Market*, the British version of a Central European operetta (the New York run had begun in September 1913). Words: Harry B. Smith [special "dance" words by Arthur Behim]. Music: Jerome (D.) Kern. Pub.: Leo. Feist, Inc., N.Y, 1914. (Apparently the song was interpolated again in the New York production of *The Laughing Husband*, another Continental operetta in a new London guise; New York opening was in February 1914.)

Alphabetical List of Songwriters and Lyricists

Harold R. Atteridge (1886–1938): lyricist and librettist for numerous Broadway musicals to 1934, including various editions of *The Passing Show*, the 1927 *Ziegfeld Follies*, some of Jolson's big shows and several Shubert extravaganzas.

Ernest R. Ball (1878–1927): songwriter and vaudeville pianist; wrote such standards as "Will You Love Me in December as You Do in May," "Let the Rest of the World Go By" and "Love Me and the World Is Mine," and such Irish-American classics as "Mother Machree" and "When Irish Eyes Are Smiling."

Irving Berlin (1888–1989): Russian-born; America's most honored popular tunesmith (also a music publisher and theater owner); author of some 1500 songs between 1907 and 1966, for Tin Pan Alley, 19 stage shows and 18 movies; especially revered for such patriotic numbers as "God Bless America" and such timeless perennials as "White Christmas"; 1914, the year of this anthology, saw the production of *Watch Your Step*, the first Broadway show with a score completely by Berlin.

Henry Blossom (1866–1919): playwright; lyricist and librettist of several Victor Herbert shows, including *Mlle. Modiste* (1905), *The Red Mill* (1906), *The Only Girl* (1914) and *Eileen* (1917); also a Broadway producer.

J. Keirn Brennan (1873–1948): singer; lyricist for Broadway musicals to 1930.

Harry Carroll (1892–1962): songwriter, pianist, vaudeville entertainer, active to at least 1930; other major songs include "The Trail of the Lonesome Pine" and "I'm Always Chasing Rainbows" (adaptation of a Chopin melody), the first enormous song hit based on a classical theme.

Ivan Caryll (1861–1921); Belgian-born, real name Félix Tilken; operetta composer active in London and New York up to the time of his death; major N.Y hit was "My Beautiful Lady" from *The Pink Lady* (1911).

J. M. Cavanass (1842–1919): newspaper editor; versified "By the Waters of Minnetonka" at Lieurance's request.

Grant Clarke (1891–1931): librettist for musicals and clever lyricist of novelty and specialty songs for stage and screen, including "He'd Have to Get Under," "Ragtime Cowboy Joe," "Second Hand Rose," "Dirty Hands, Dirty Face" and "Am I Blue?"

Hermann E. Darewski (1883–1947): English, born in Russia; songwriter and bandleader; house composer for the London publisher Francis, Day & Hunter from 1906; wrote a number of popular West End revues in the 1910s.

Walter Donovan (1888–1964): songwriter, pianist; also wrote "One Dozen Roses."

John Valentine Eppel (1871–1931): orchestra leader in Chicago.

Arthur Fields (1888–1953): Songwriter, lyricist, actor, publisher.

William H(enry) Gardner (1865–1932): lyricist of religious and uplifting songs.

John Golden (1874–1955): lyricist, songwriter, playwright, theatrical director and producer; his two hit lyrics are "Goodbye, Girls, I'm Through" and "Poor Butterfly"; major Broadway producer from 1916 to 1949; a Broadway theater bears his name.

W(illiam) C(hristopher) Handy (1873–1958): composer, musician, music teacher, orchestra leader, music publisher, anthologist; while in Memphis, associated with the earliest published commercial blues ("The Memphis Blues," "The St. Louis Blues," "Beale Street Blues"); active in New York from 1918; toured with orchestras; honored as "Father of the Blues."

Victor Herbert (1859–1924): cellist, orchestra leader, composer of operettas and shows; born in Ireland, studied in Germany; wrote over 40 shows for Broadway, including *The Fortune Teller* (1898), *Babes in Toyland* (1903), *Mlle. Modiste* (1905), *The Red Mill* (1906), *Naughty Marietta* (1910), *Sweethearts* (1913) and *Eileen* (1917); dozens of his songs are American standards.

Jerome (David) Kern (1885–1945): one of the greatest Broadway and Hollywood songwriters; up through 1914, the year of this anthology, he chiefly supplied songs to be interpolated in other composers' shows, the best of these being "They Didn't Believe Me" and "You're Here and I'm Here" (both 1914); from 1915 to 1939 he wrote numerous successful Broadway musicals and operettas, including the epoch-making *Show Boat* (1927); from 1935 to his death he wrote many film scores, winning Academy Awards for the songs "The Way You Look Tonight" and "The Last Time I Saw Paris" (the latter not specifically written for the movies).

Thurlow (Weed) Lieurance (1878–1963): classical composer (opera, instrumental works); collector and adapter of American Indian music, employed by the U.S. government from 1903 on.

Frederic Knight Logan (1871–1928): composer, conductor.

Jack (Francis) Mahoney (1882–1945): lyricist, particularly of specialty songs for stars.

Hebert Reynolds (1867–1933): pseudonym of Michael E. Rourke; born in England; lyricist; did English versions of several Viennese operettas.

Caro Roma (1866–1937): pseudonym of Carrie Northey; writer of salon-style inspirational songs and imitations of black folksongs.

Clinton Scollard (1860–1932): poet, professor of English literature.

J(ames) R(oyce) Shannon (1881–1946): songwriter, lyricist, actor, theater executive; represented in this volume not only by "Too-Ra-Loo-Ra-Loo-Ral" (words and music) but also by "The Missouri Waltz" (words added to an earlier instrumental version).

Rudolf Sieczyński (1879–1952): Viennese composer and lyricist.

Harry B(ache) Smith (1860–1936): one of the most distinguished Broadway lyricists and librettists; worked with Victor Herbert on *The Fortune Teller* (1898) and *The Enchantress* (1911) and with Reginald De Koven on *Robin Hood* (1890); did English versions of Viennese operettas; also an actor.

Oley Speaks (1874–1948): composer; singer; most famous for "On the Road to Mandalay."

Percy Wenrich (1887–1952); songwriter, rag composer, pianist; specialized in old-fashioned Americana, such as "When You Wore a Tulip" (in the present volume), "Put On Your Old Grey Bonnet" and "Moonlight Bay."

R. P. Weston: same as the lyricist and librettist of the Broadway musical *Tell Her the Truth* in 1932?

Notes on the Song Texts

"*The Aba Daba Honeymoon*": Note the use of "swing" and "swinging" in a way that seems to foreshadow the use of those words in the 1930s and later.

"*By the Beautiful Sea*": "Marcelling hair" means waving women's hair with hot irons in a beauty parlor (process named for a French hairdresser of the 1890s).

"*By the Waters of Minnetonka*": The Indian word of the title is said to mean "large round lake" in a Sioux language.

"*Goodbye, Girls, I'm Through*": The "Path of Flowers" is a traditional Chinese literary phrase denoting amorous dalliance.

"*He's a Devil in His Own Home Town*": "Heckers" was an early twentieth-century term for rustics (from their saying "By heck!"); perhaps also a euphemism for "hellers" (hellions, hell-raisers).

"*The St. Louis Blues*": "Jelly Roll" refers to a sweetheart or sex partner; "Cairo" is, of course, the city in Illinois; "maself" pronounced the Southern way without the *l*-sound is a perfect rhyme for "Jeff"; "stove pipe brown" is a dark-skinned black man; "Dimon Joseph" is the Diamond-Joseph railroad line; "on the dot" usually means exact, punctual (ironic or different meaning here?).

"*Too-Ra-Loo-Ra-Loo-Ral*": The name of the show in which it was introduced, *Shameen Dhu*, is equivalent to "black-haired Jimmy."

"*Wien, du Stadt meiner Träume*": FULL LITERAL TRANSLATION OF TEXT—1. My heart and my mind constantly rave about Vienna alone, about Vienna as it weeps and it laughs. There I know my way around, there I'm right at home by day and even more at night. And no one remains indifferent, whether young or old, who knows Vienna as it really is. If I should ever have to leave the beautiful place, my longing would never end. (REFRAIN:) Then I would hear from a great distance a song that sounds and sings, that allures and attracts. Vienna, Vienna, you alone shall constantly be the city of my dreams—there where the old houses stand, there where the lovely girls walk—Vienna, Vienna, you alone shall constantly be the city of my dreams—there where I am happy and blissful, is Vienna, is Vienna, my Vienna!

2. At every spree—well, you know it—I am always right there. I maintain my good spirits till way into the wee hours—then it's all the same to me. And when I then sit down to my wine with a companion and an arm embraces me longingly; when mysteriously and softly, in praise of my homeland, a Strauss waltz rings out: (REFRAIN:) Then I would hear, etc.

3. Whether I want to or not, but very late I hope, I must someday leave the world behind. There must come a parting from love and wine, because everything passes away just as it comes. Ah, that will be delightful, I won't need to walk, for I'll fly up to heaven. There I'll take a seat, look down toward Vienna, and St. Stephen's [the cathedral] will send up a greeting. (REFRAIN:) Then I would hear, etc.

4. In storm and distress, threatened on all sides by enemies, Austria stands upright and noble, defended round about by heroes with gleaming sword and wearing protective iron armor! Where music and song resounded in peace, now trumpet signals blare! Out of their gentle character there grows strong and flourishing a race of heroes without number! (REFRAIN:) And then when in the field slumber flees from you, let the song sound softly from afar: Vienna, Vienna, you alone, etc.

ABA DABA HONEYMOON

RUTH ROYE'S SENSATIONAL NOVELTY SONG HIT

RUBY **Raymond** and **Heider** FRED
"THE AMBITIOUS STREET URCHINS"

As Featured By
RUTH ROYE
The PRINCESS of RAGTIME
14 Consecutive weeks at
The PALACE THEATRE
New York

by
ARTHUR FIELDS
and
WALTER DONOVAN

5

Leo. Feist New York

4 The Aba Daba Honeymoon

10   By the Beautiful Sea

16 *By the Waters of Minnetonka*

Sung by
GEORGE MACFARLANE.

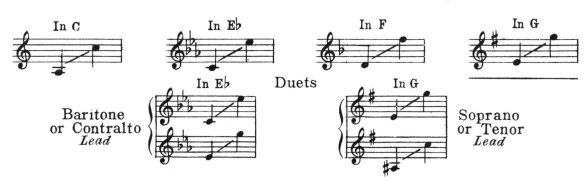

CAN'T YO' HEAH ME CALLIN'
CAROLINE
···SONG···

LYRIC BY

WM. H. GARDNER
Author of "THE CROWN OF LIFE," "LIST TO THE VOICE DIVINE" etc.

Music by

CARO ROMA
Composer of "RESIGNATION", "I COME TO THEE,"
"O, LORD REMEMBER ME", "THE WANDERING ONE" *(Song Cycle)* etc.

Solo 60 Cents   Duet 75 Cents

M. WITMARK & SONS.

NEW YORK   SAN FRANCISCO
LONDON   MELBOURNE.

Can't Yo' Heah Me Callin'
CAROLINE

I miss yo' in de mo'nin', when ole Bob-White gives his call,
    Caroline, Caroline,
I miss yo' at de sunset, when de evenin' shadows fall,
    Caroline, Caroline;
I miss yo' when de moonbeams out on de ribber shine,
Oh can't yo' heah me callin' fo' yo', Caroline.

    Can't yo' heah me callin', Caroline,
    It's mah heart a-callin' dine.
    Lordy, how I miss yo,' gal o' mine,
    Wish dat I could kiss yo' Caroline!
    Ain't no use now fo' de sun to shine,
        Caroline, Caroline,
    Can't yo' heah mah lips a-sayin',
    Can't yo' heah mah soul a-prayin',
    Can't yo' heah me callin', Caroline.

I miss yo' when de Robin is a-whistlin' out his tune,
    Caroline, Caroline,
I miss yo' when de roses are a-bloomin' all of June,
    Caroline, Caroline;
I miss yer hand a-stealin' so trustin' like in mine,
Oh can't yo' heah me callin' fo' yo', Caroline.

Wm H. Gardner

Can't Yo' Heah Me Callin'
Caroline

Lyric by
Wm H. GARDNER

Music by
CARO ROMA

Copyright MCMXIV by M. Witmark & Sons
International Copyright Secured

Can't Yo' Heah Me Callin'

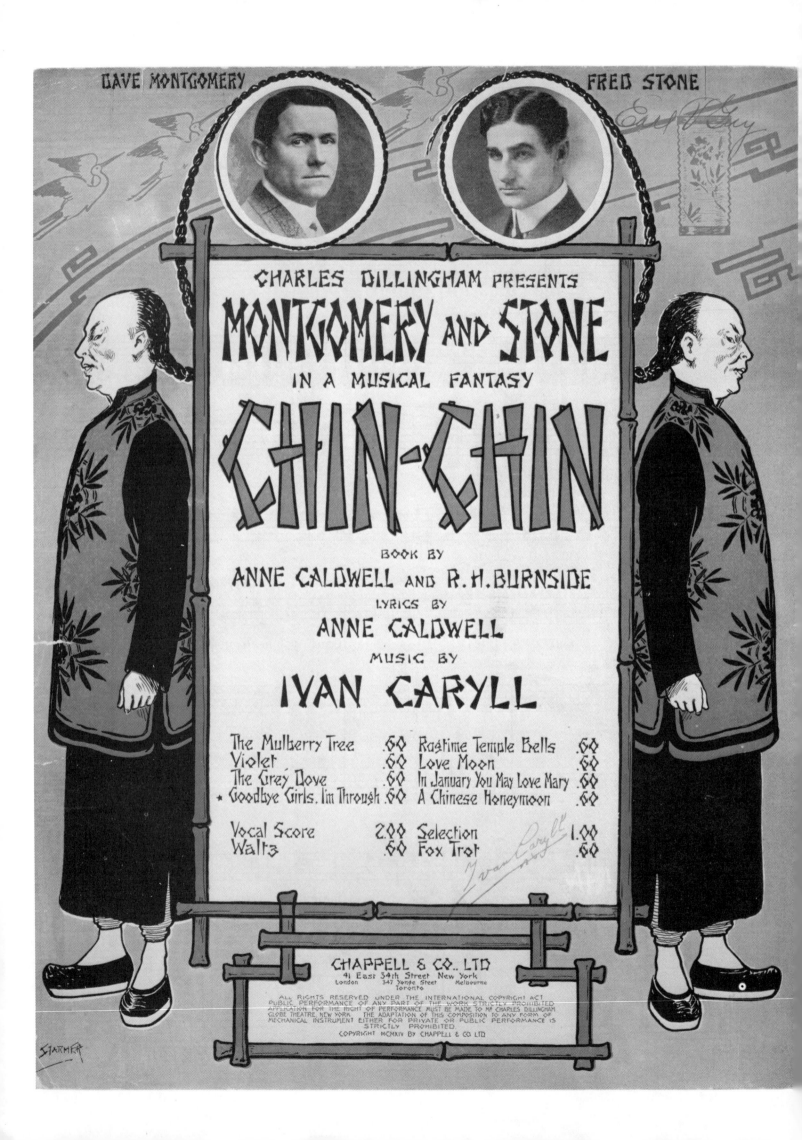

Goodbye Girls I'm Through
SONG

Words by
JOHN GOLDEN

Music by
IVAN CARYLL

Copyright MCMXIV by Chappell & Co. L't'd.
All rights reserved.

24 Goodbye, Girls, I'm Through

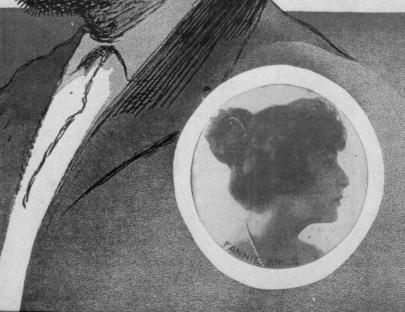

He's a Devil in His Own Home Town   29

30 *He's a Devil in His Own Home Town*

HE'S A RAG PICKER

by IRVING BERLIN

Copyright MCMXIV by Waterson, Berlin & Snyder Co.
Copyright Canada, MCMXIV by Waterson, Berlin & Snyder Co.
International Copyright Secured.

36 He's a Rag Picker

I Want To Go Back To Michigan
(DOWN ON THE FARM)

Words and Music by
Irving Berlin

Copyright MCMXIV by Waterson, Berlin & Snyder Co.
Copyright Canada MCMXIV by Waterson, Berlin & Snyder Co.
International Copyright Secured.

I Want to Go Back to Michigan

40 I Want to Go Back to Michigan

I Want to Go Back to Michigan 41

SUNG BY

MR. CHAUNCEY OLCOTT

IN

THE HEART OF PADDY WHACK

A LITTLE BIT OF HEAVEN SHURE THEY CALL IT IRELAND

(HOW IRELAND GOT IT'S NAME)

SONG

LYRIC BY

J. KEIRN BRENNAN

MUSIC BY

ERNEST R. BALL

Composer of "MOTHER MACHREE", "WHO KNOWS?", "MY DEAR",
"WHEN IRISH EYES ARE SMILING", "IN THE GARDEN OF MY HEART,"
"TILL THE SANDS OF THE DESERT GROW COLD", "IRISH EYES OF LOVE" etc.

Price 60 cents.

M. WITMARK & SONS,

NEW YORK · CHICAGO · LONDON.

A Little Bit Of Heaven
Shure They Call It Ireland

Have you ever heard the story of how Ireland got its name?
I'll tell you so you'll understand from whence old Ireland came;
No wonder that we're proud of that dear land across the sea,
For here's the way me dear old mother told the tale to me:

Shure, a little bit of Heaven fell from out the sky one day,
And nestled on the ocean in a spot so far away;
And when the angels found it, shure it looked so sweet and fair,
They said, "Suppose we leave it, for it looks so peaceful there."
So they sprinkled it with star dust just to make the shamrocks grow,
'Tis the only place you'll find them, no matter where you go;
Then they dotted it with silver, to make its lakes so grand,
And when they had it finished, shure they called it Ireland.

'Tis a dear old land of fairies and of wond'rous wishing wells,
And no where else on God's green earth have they such lakes and dells!
No wonder that the angels loved its Shamrock-bordered shore,
'Tis a little bit of Heaven, and I love it more and more.

J. Keirn Brennan

46   A Little Bit of Heaven

HUSH-A-BYE, MA BABY
MISSOURI
WALTZ
SONG

IMPERIAL SONGRECORD No. 9235

From an Original Melody

Produced by

John Valentine Eppel

REVISED EDITION

ARRANGED FOR PIANO BY

FREDERIC KNIGHT LOGAN

Price 60c.

ALSO PUBLISHED AS FOLLOWS	
DUET { SOP. AND ALTO OR TENOR AND BARITONE	60C
MALE QUARTETTE	60C
MIXED QUARTETTE	60C

F.J.A FORSTER MUSIC PUBLISHER 529 S.WABASH AV. CHICAGO, ILL.

50 The Missouri Waltz

Simple Melody

Ernesta, Algy and Chorus

Words and Music by IRVING BERLIN

ERNESTA

The diff-'rent lays of now-a-days All set my brain a-whirl. They're
In days of yore, be-fore the war, When hearts now old were young. At

not the kind of songs they sang When moth-er was a girl, Your
home each night by fire - light Those dear old songs were sung_ Sweet

spoon-y rags and coon-y drags All made my poor heart ache, Bring
mel - o - dies their mem-o-ries A - round my heart still cling, That's

Copyright 1914 by IRVING BERLIN Inc. 1571 Broadway, N.Y.
International Copyright Secured.
Copyright Canada 1914 by IRVING BERLIN Inc.
Performing Rights Reserved.

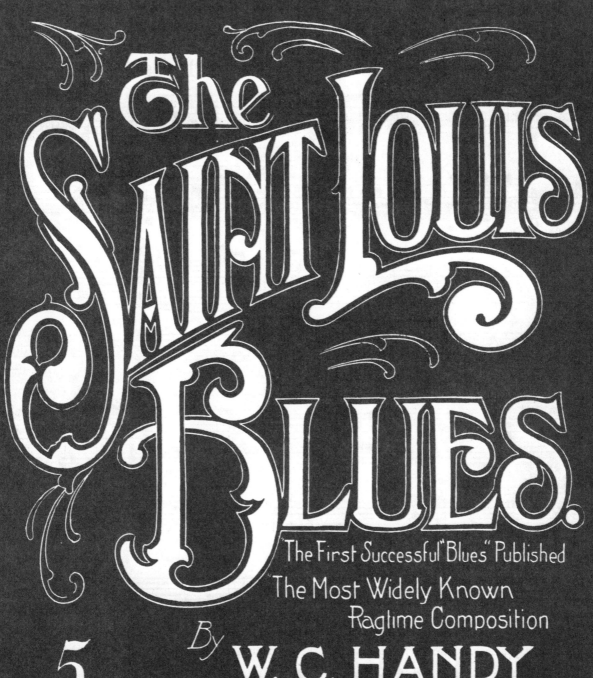

Sister Susie's Sewing Shirts For Soldiers.

Written by
R. P. Weston.

Composed by
Hermann E. Darewski.

Copyright MCMXIV, in all Countries by Francis, Day & Hunter.
Copyright MCMXIV by T. B. Harms & Francis, Day & Hunter, N.Y.
All Rights Reserved.   International Copyright Secured.

Sister Susie's Sewing Shirts for Soldiers

66 *Sister Susie's Sewing Shirts for Soldiers*

Sylvia

Clinton Scollard
Oley Speaks

Sylvia's hair is like the night, Touched with glancing starry beams; Such a face as drifts thro' dreams, This is Sylvia to the sight.

Copyright, 1914, by G. Schirmer

They Didn't Believe Me.

Words by
HERBERT REYNOLDS

Music by
JEROME KERN.

Copyright MCMXIV by T. B. Harms & Francis, Day & Hunter, N.Y.
All stage rights reserved by the Composer.   International Copyright Secured.

They Didn't Believe Me   73

They Didn't Believe Me

This is the Life

Successfully Introduced By
AL. JOLSON

by Irving Berlin

WATERSON·BERLIN & SNYDER CO
MUSIC PUBLISHERS
112 WEST 38TH ST. NEW YORK

THIS IS THE LIFE.

IRVING BERLIN

Copyright MCMXIV, by Waterson, Berlin & Snyder Co.
Copyright, Canada, MCMXIV, by Waterson, Berlin & Snyder Co.
International Copyright Secured.

80 This Is the Life

TOO-RA-LOO-RA-LOO-RAL

That's An Irish Lullaby

LYRIC and MUSIC BY

J. R. SHANNON

PUBLISHED IN THE FOLLOWING ARRANGEMENTS

Vocal Solo, C–E♭–F–G . . . . each .50	Piano Solo (Gotham Classics No. 85) .50
Vocal Duet, E♭–G . . . . each .60	3 Part Mixed (SAB) 15
2 Part (SA or TB) 15	4 Part Mixed (SATB) 15
3 Part Treble (SSA) 15	Accordion Solo (Bass Clef) 50
4 Part Treble (SSAA) 16	Vocal Orchestration, F–C . . . . each .75
4 Part Male (TTBB) 15	Dance Orchestration (Fox Trot) 75
Band 1.00	

THE WITMARK BLACK AND WHITE SERIES

WHEN PERFORMING THIS COMPOSITION KINDLY GIVE ALL
PROGRAM CREDITS TO

M. Witmark & Sons

NEW YORK

PRINTED IN U.S.A

84 Too-Ra-Loo-Ra-Loo-Ral

When You're Away

RUTH

Lyric by
HENRY BLOSSOM

Music by
VICTOR HERBERT

Though time may let us sometimes forget, Until, with but a sigh, The mem'ries of a passionate love Turn ashen cold and die. For

Copyright MCMXIV by M. Witmark & Sons
International Copyright Secured

88 When You're Away

When You're Away 89

When You Wore A Tulip
and
I Wore A Big Red Rose

Words by
JACK MAHONEY

Music by
PERCY WENRICH

Tempo di marcia

Till ready

I met you in a gar-den in an old Ken-tuck-y town, The sun was shin-ing down, you wore a ging-ham gown; I kissed you, as I placed a yel-low tul-ip in your hair, Up-

The love you vowed to cher-ish has not fal-tered thro' the years, You ban-ish all my fears, your voice like mus-ic cheers, You are the same sweet girl I knew in hap-py days of old, Your

Copyright MCMXIV by LEO. FEIST, Inc., Feist Building, N.Y.
International Copyright Secured and Reserved
London — Ascherberg, Hopwood & Crew, Limited.

Frau Lisl Breycha in Verehrung gewidmet.

Wien, du Stadt meiner Träume.
Wienerlied.

Dr. Rudolf Sieczyński, Op. 1.

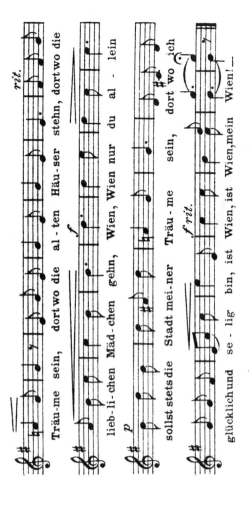

2.
Bei jeder Gaudé,
Na, sie wissen's ja e,
Bin ich allemal gleich dabei.
Ich b'halt mein Hamur
Bis spat in der Fruah,
Mir ist alles dann einerlei.
Und wenn ich beim Wein
Dann sitze zu zwein,
Und sehnend ein Arm mich umschlingt,
Wenn heimlich und leis
Der Heimat zum Preis
Ein Straussischer Walzer erklingt:
Refrain: Dann hört ich *u. s. w.*

3.
Ob ich will oder net,
Nur hoff ich, recht spät
Muß ich einmal fort von der Welt.
Geschieden muß sein
Von Liebe und Wein,
Weil alles, wie's kommt, auch vergeht.
Ah, das wird ganz schön,
Ich brauch ja nicht z'gehn,
Ich flieg doch in' Himmel hinauf,
Dort setz ich mich hin,
Schau runter auf Wien,
Der Steffel, der grüßt ja herauf.
Refrain: Dann hört ich *u. s. w.*

4.
In Sturm und in Not, von Feinden umdroht,
Steht Österreich aufrecht und hehr.
Von Heiden umwehrt mit funkelndem Schwert
In eiserner, schirmender Wehr!
Wo Lied und Gesang im Frieden erklang,
Ertönt jetzt Trompetensignal!
Aus sanftem Gemüt erstarkt und erblüht
Ein Heldengeschlecht ohne Zahl!
Refrain: Und wenn dann im Feld der Schlummer euch flieht,
         Ertöne leis' von ferne das Lied:
         Wien, Wien nur du allein *u. s. w.*

Text und Musik Eigentum des Verlegers.   Nachdruck verboten.

You're Here and I'm Here

CHARLES FROHMAN PRESENTS

Donald Brian

IN

The Marriage Market

LYRIC BY
HARRY B. SMITH

MUSIC BY
JEROME D. KERN

OPERATIC EDITION
LEO. FEIST NEW YORK
ASCHERBERG HOPWOOD & CREW. LTD. LONDON, ENGLAND

Also published as a
ONE-STEP, TWO-STEP & TROT
as featured by
MR. & MRS. VERNON CASTLE

102 *You're Here and I'm Here*